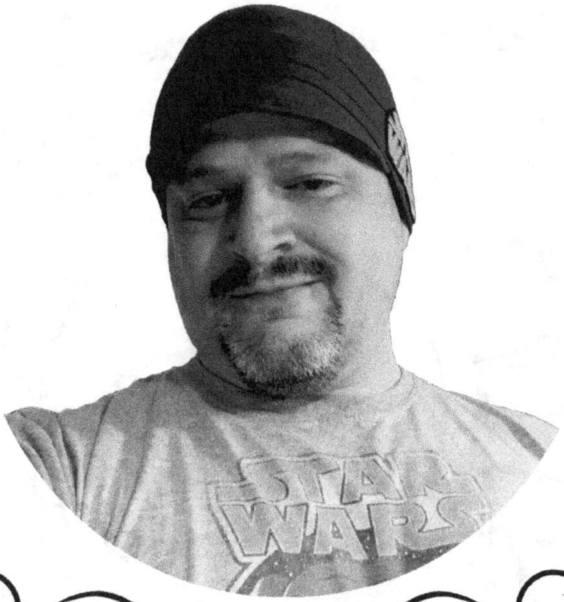

About the Artist

I am Kobold cause that is my name; and this is something I am excited to share with you. I am also a software engineer by day and freelance illustrator by night. I love pop-culture in the forms of Star Wars and Marvel, My spirit animals are George Carlin, Bruce Lee, and Captain America. An odd combination of truth, justice and a clever sense of humor.

This is my first coloring book, so i appreciate the support in purchasing this book. All of the prints in the book were made live on Twitch TV. So make sure to snap each QR code to see how the print was made as a timelapse video. I encourage you to share your colorings on social media. Make sure to use #HappyLittlePixels too.

CONTACT KOBOLD

INFO@HAPPYLITTLEPIXELS.BIZ

CONNECT ON SOCIAL MEDIA

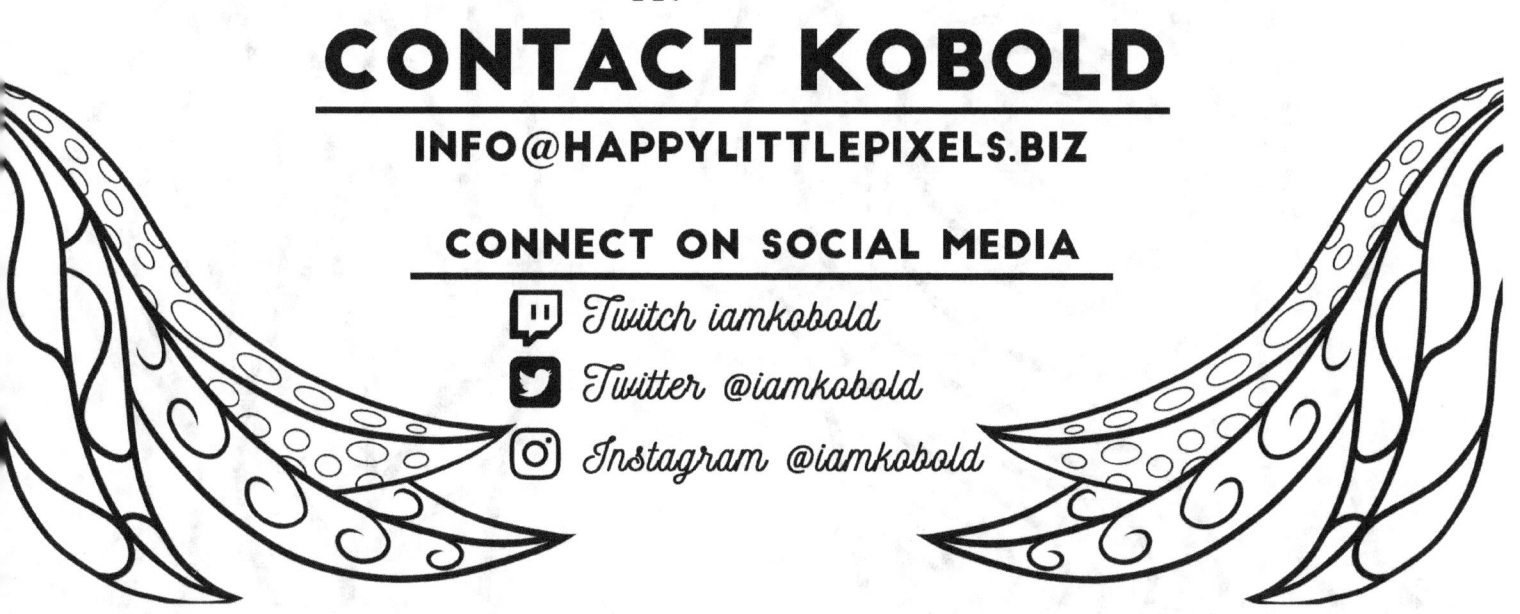

Twitch iamkobold

Twitter @iamkobold

Instagram @iamkobold

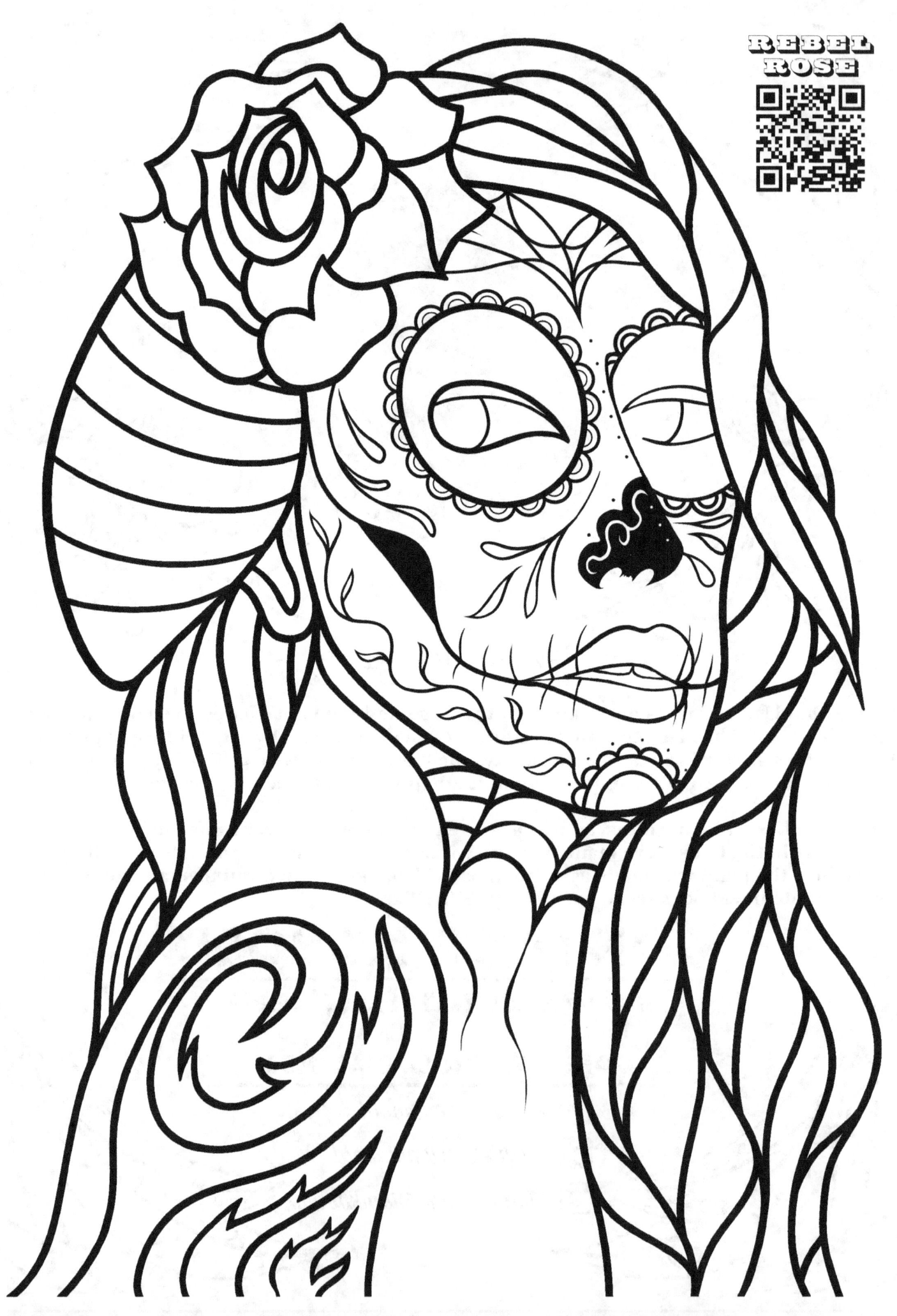
REBEL
ROSE

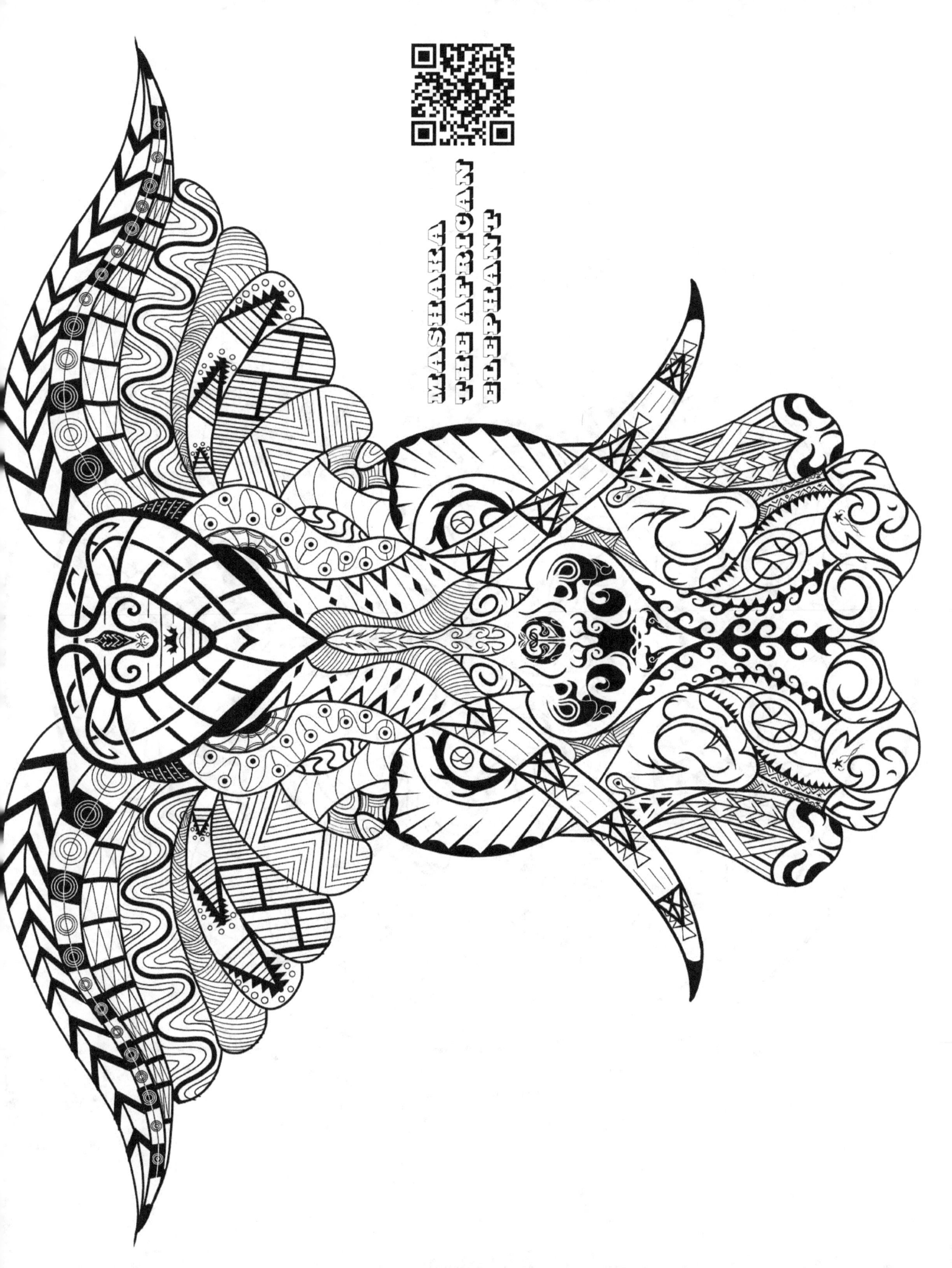

MASHARA
THE AFRICAN
ELEPHANT

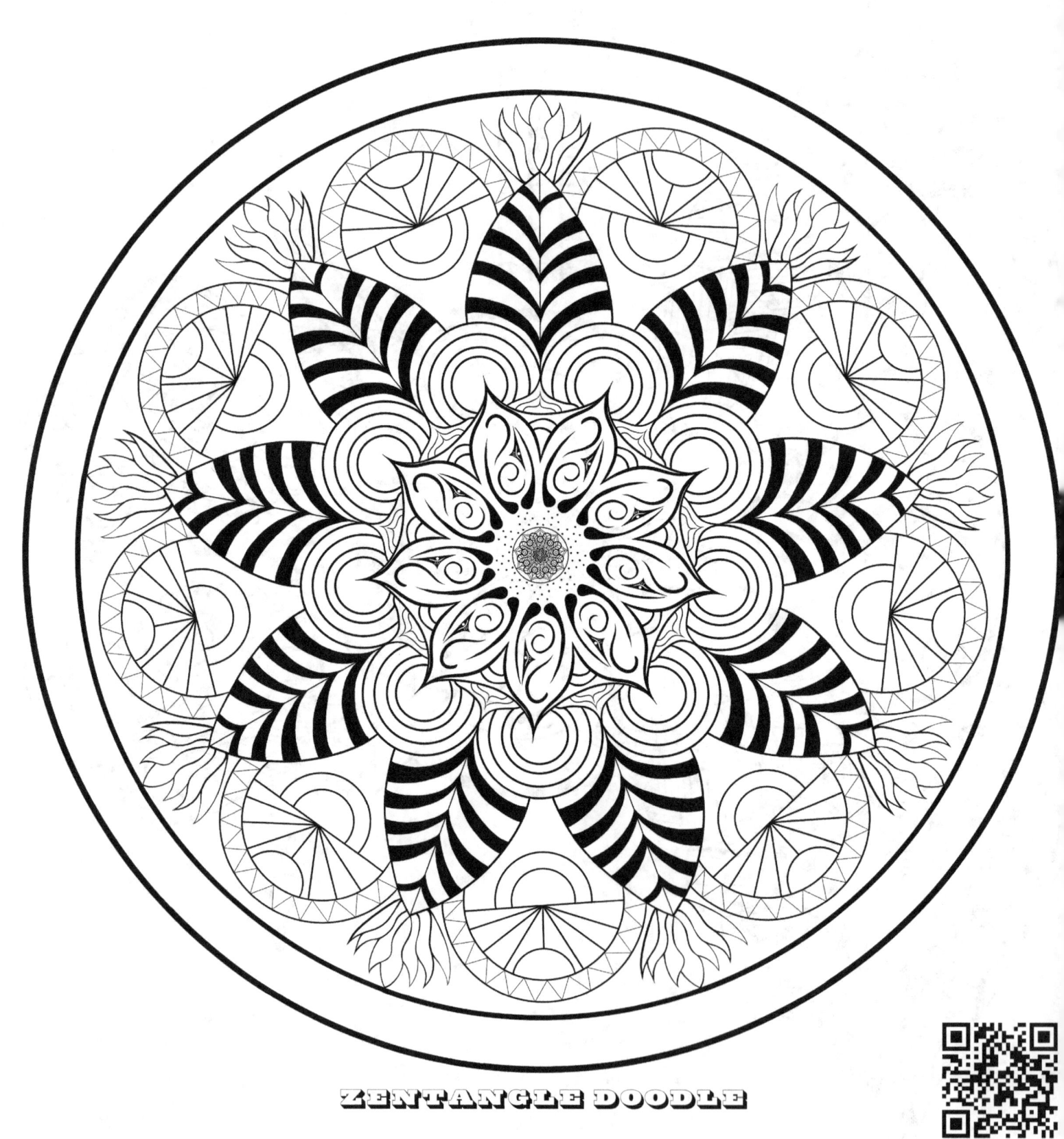

ZENTANGLE DOODLE

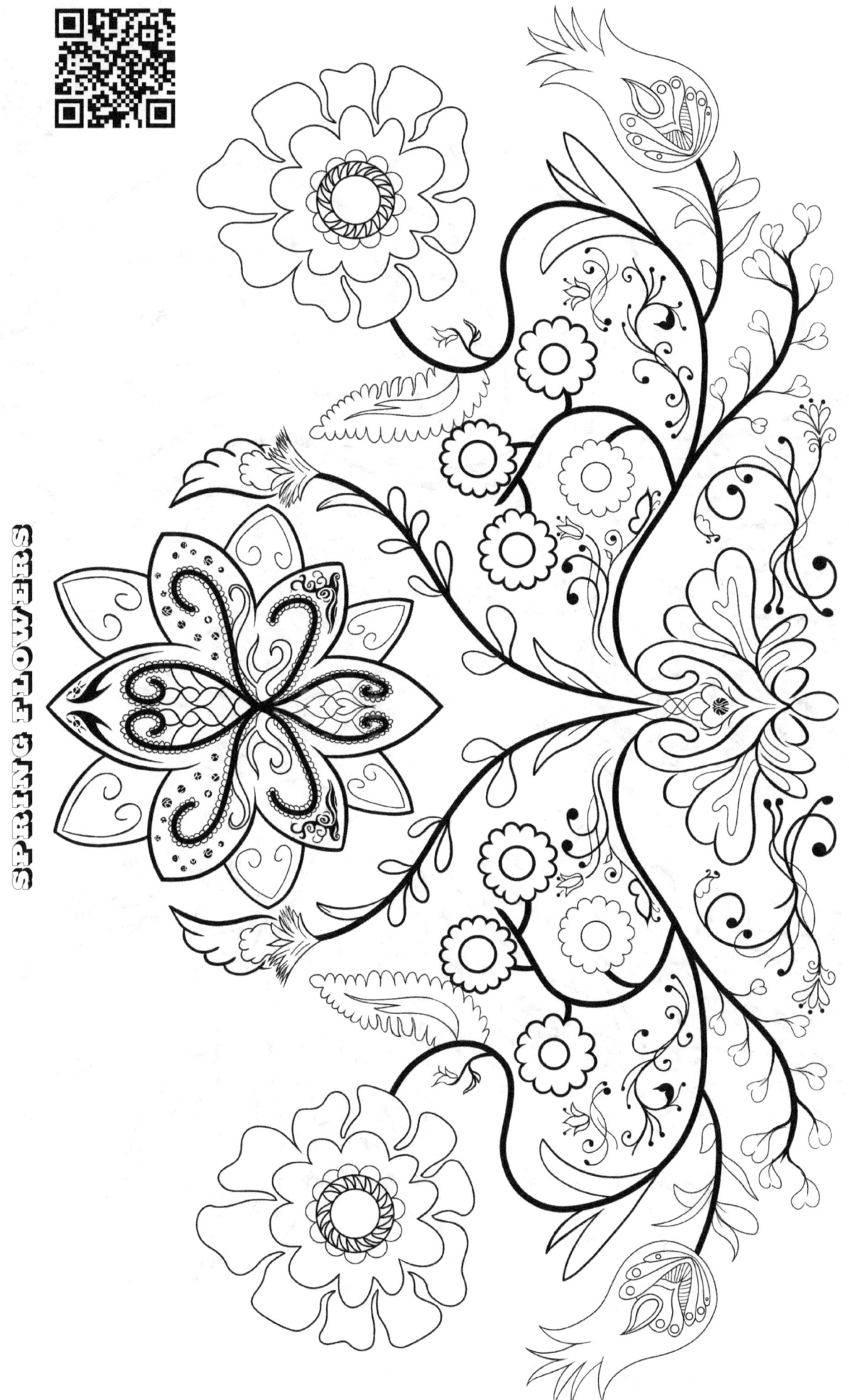

SPRING FLOWERS

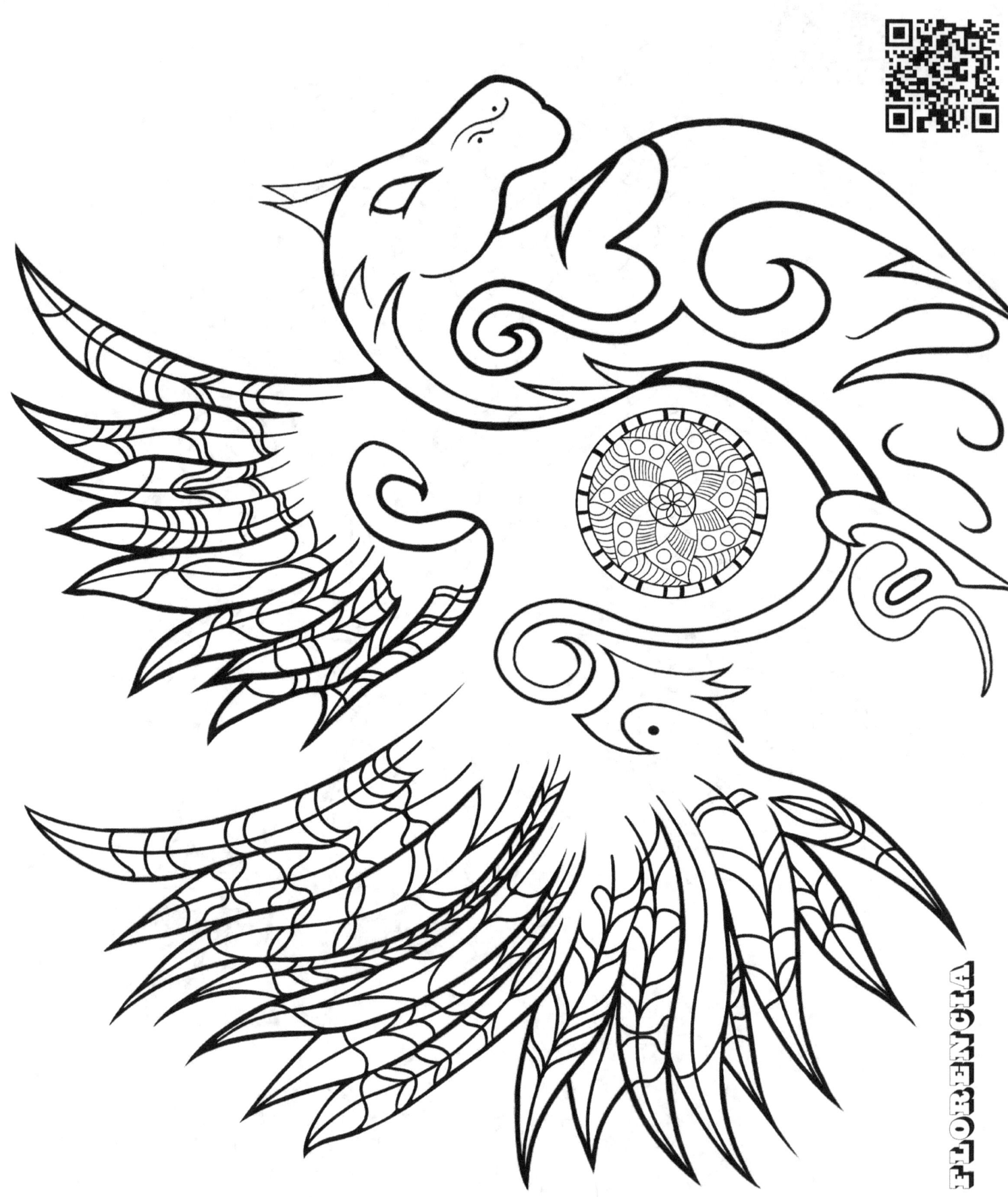

FLORENCIA

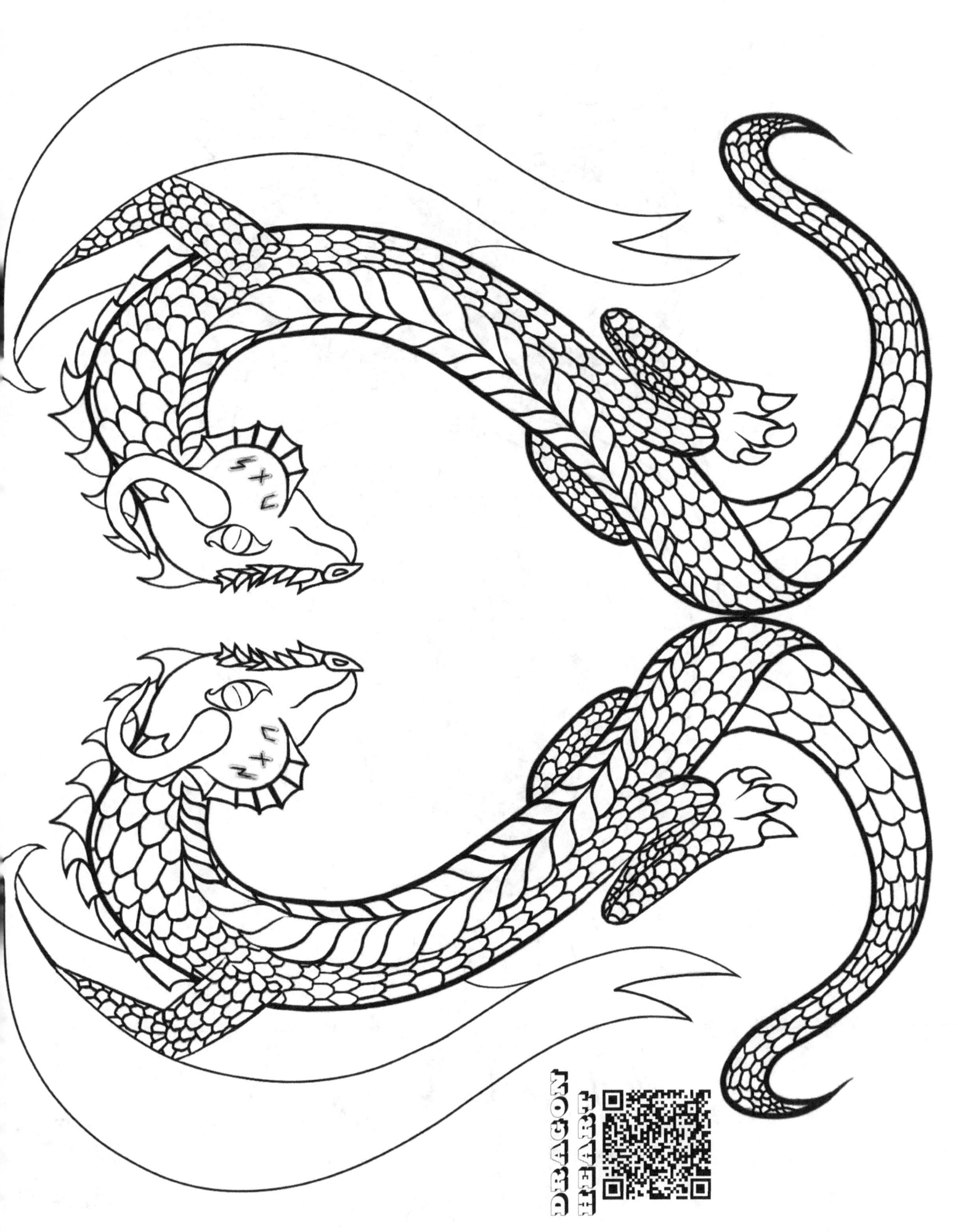

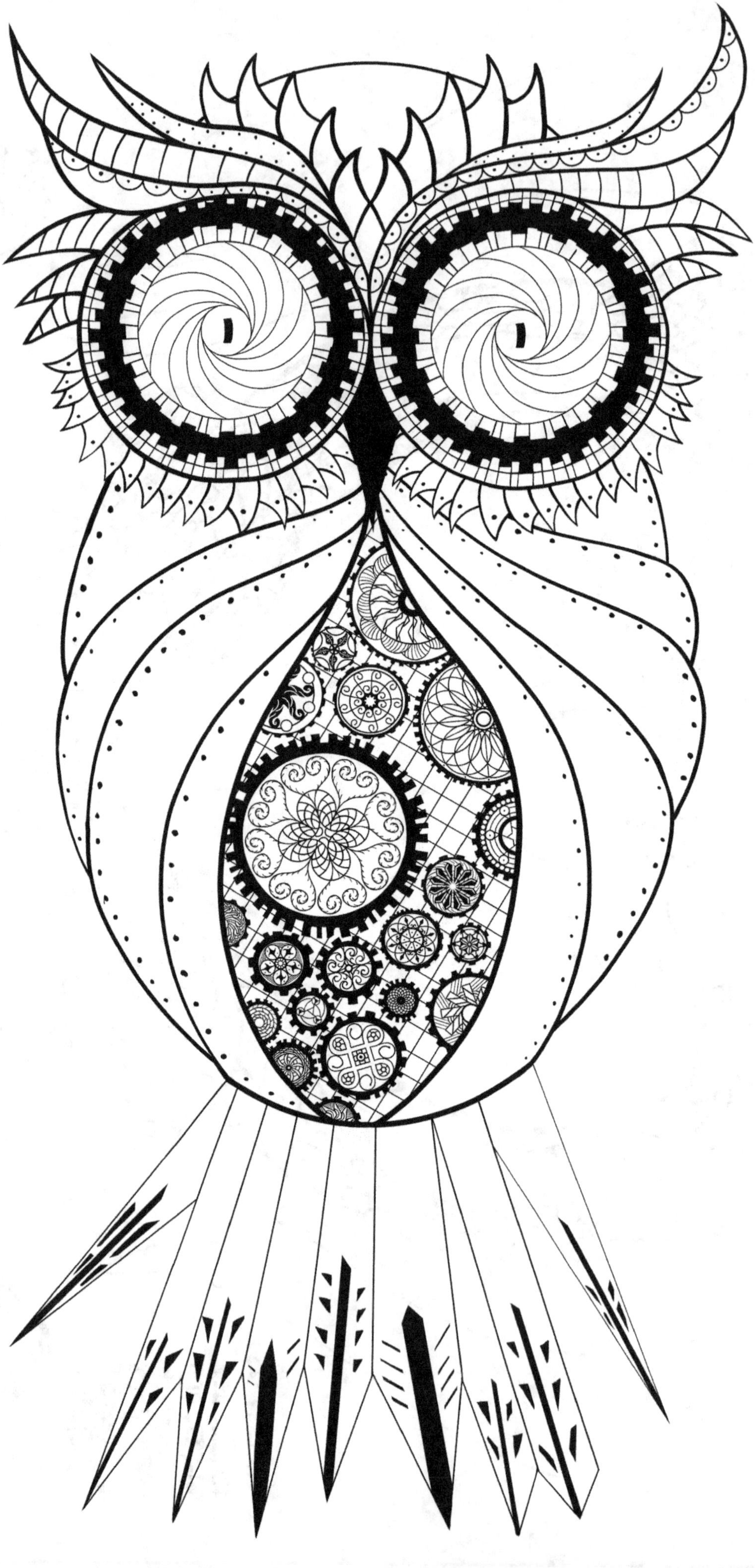

STEAMPUNK OWL

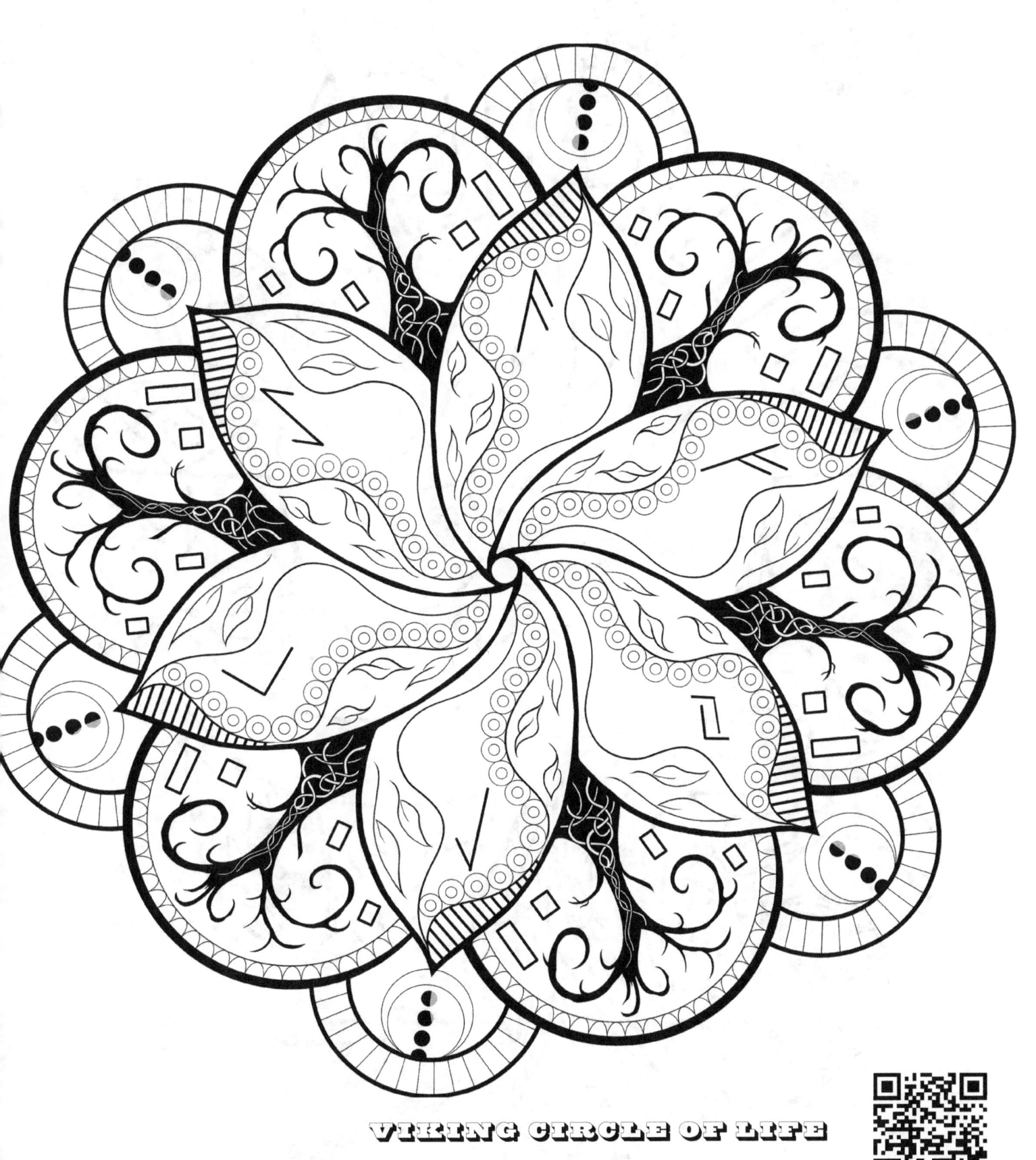

VIKING CIRCLE OF LIFE

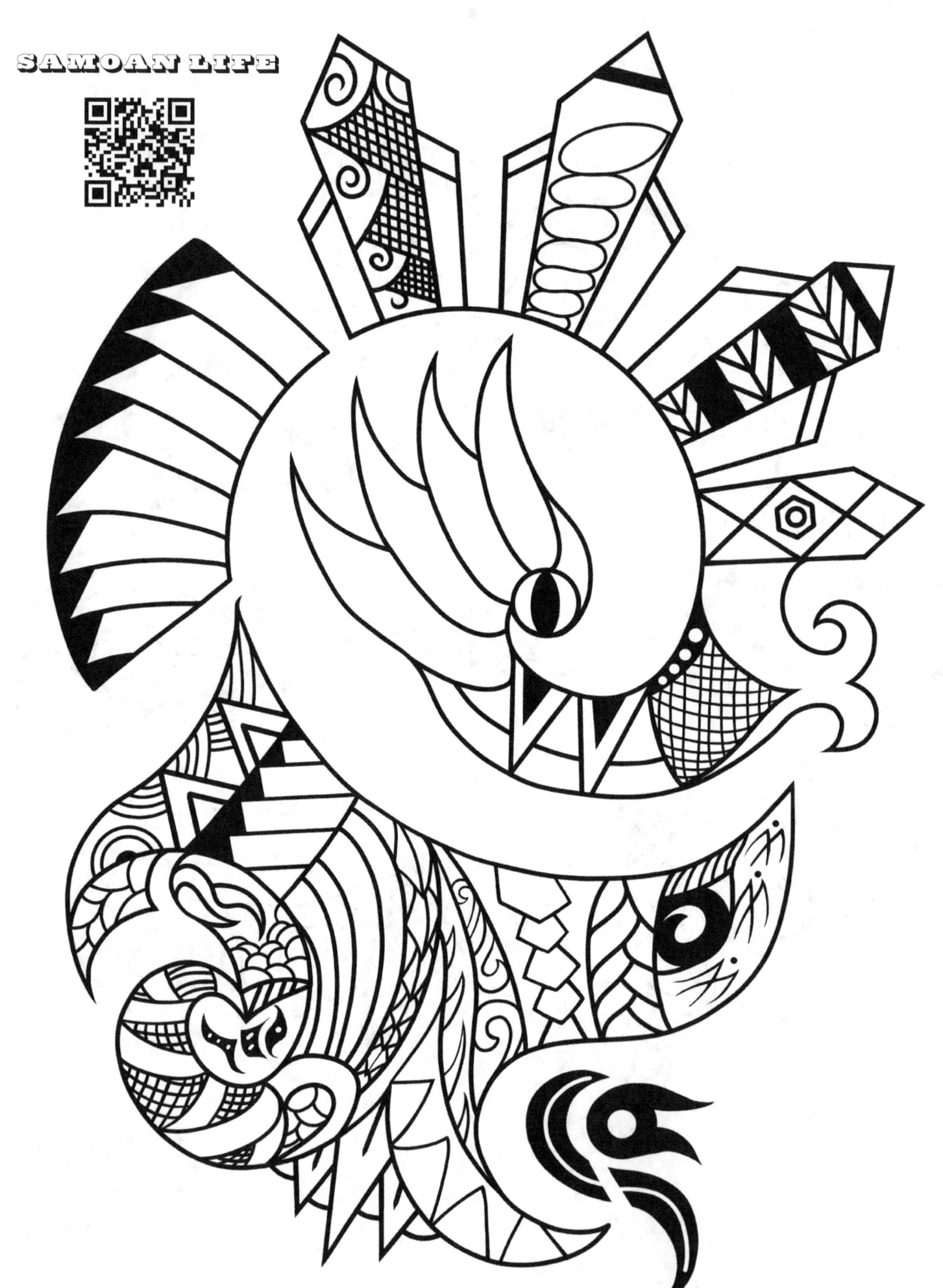

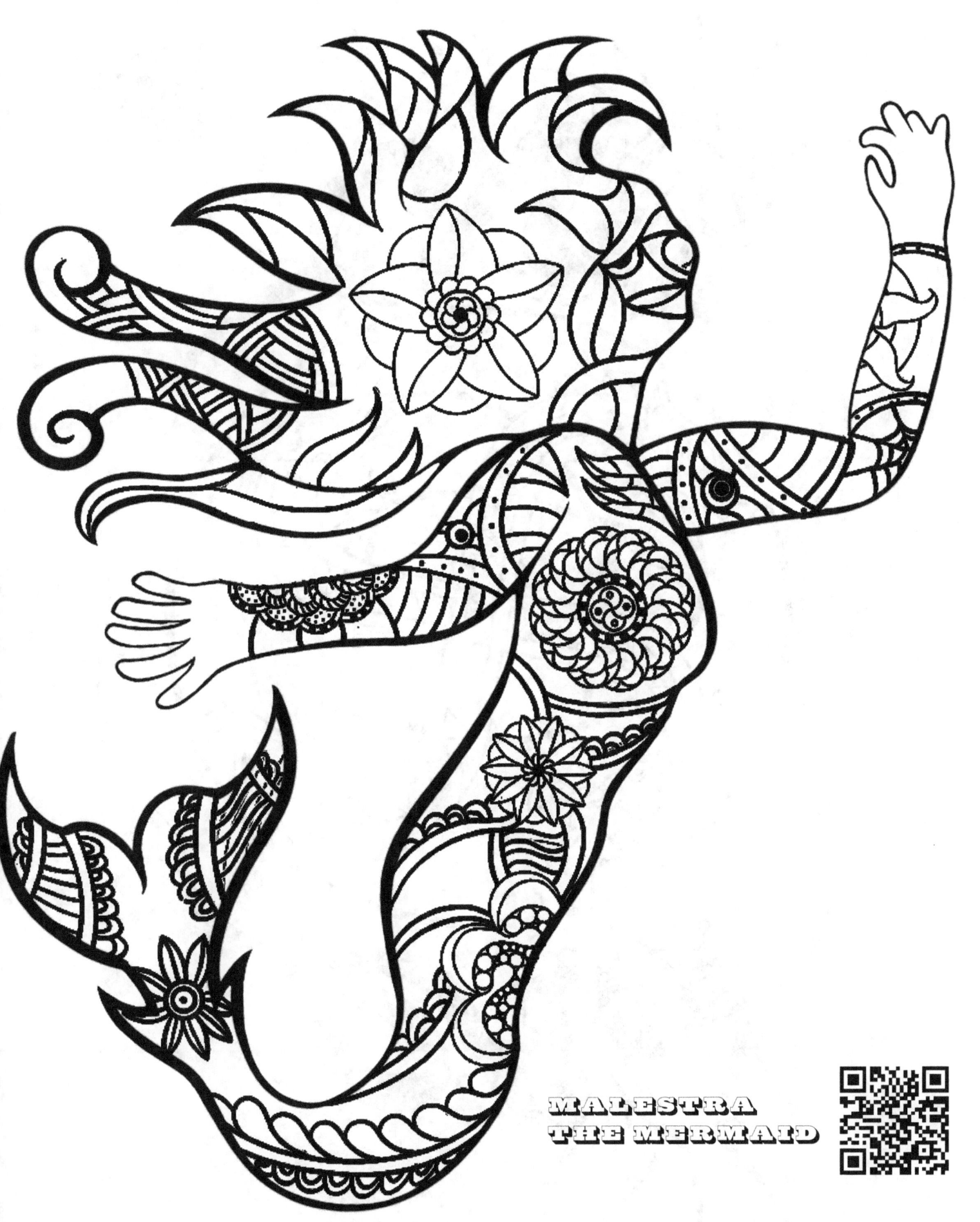

MALESTRA
THE MERMAID

SIX DRAGONS

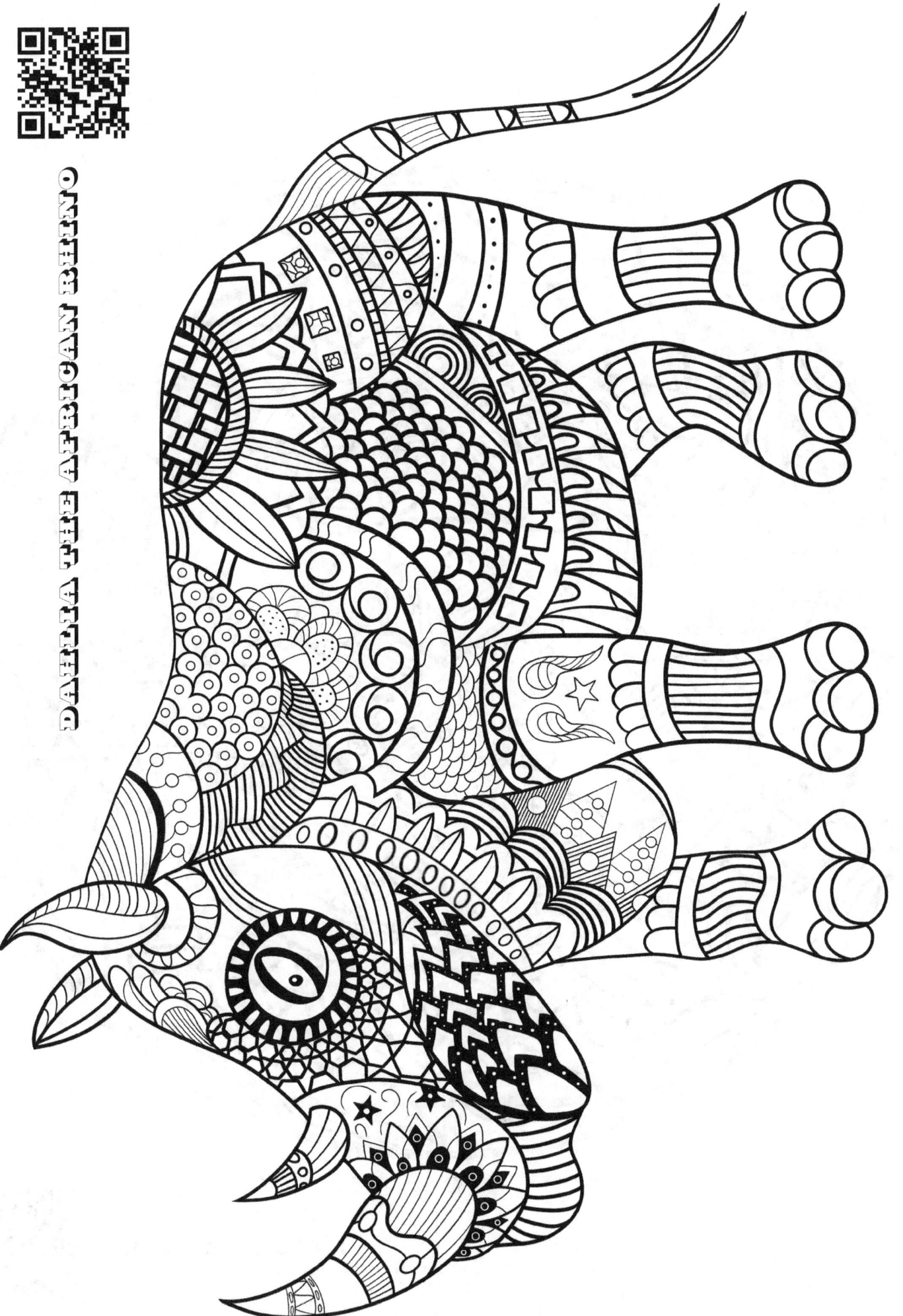

DAHLIA THE AFRICAN RHINO

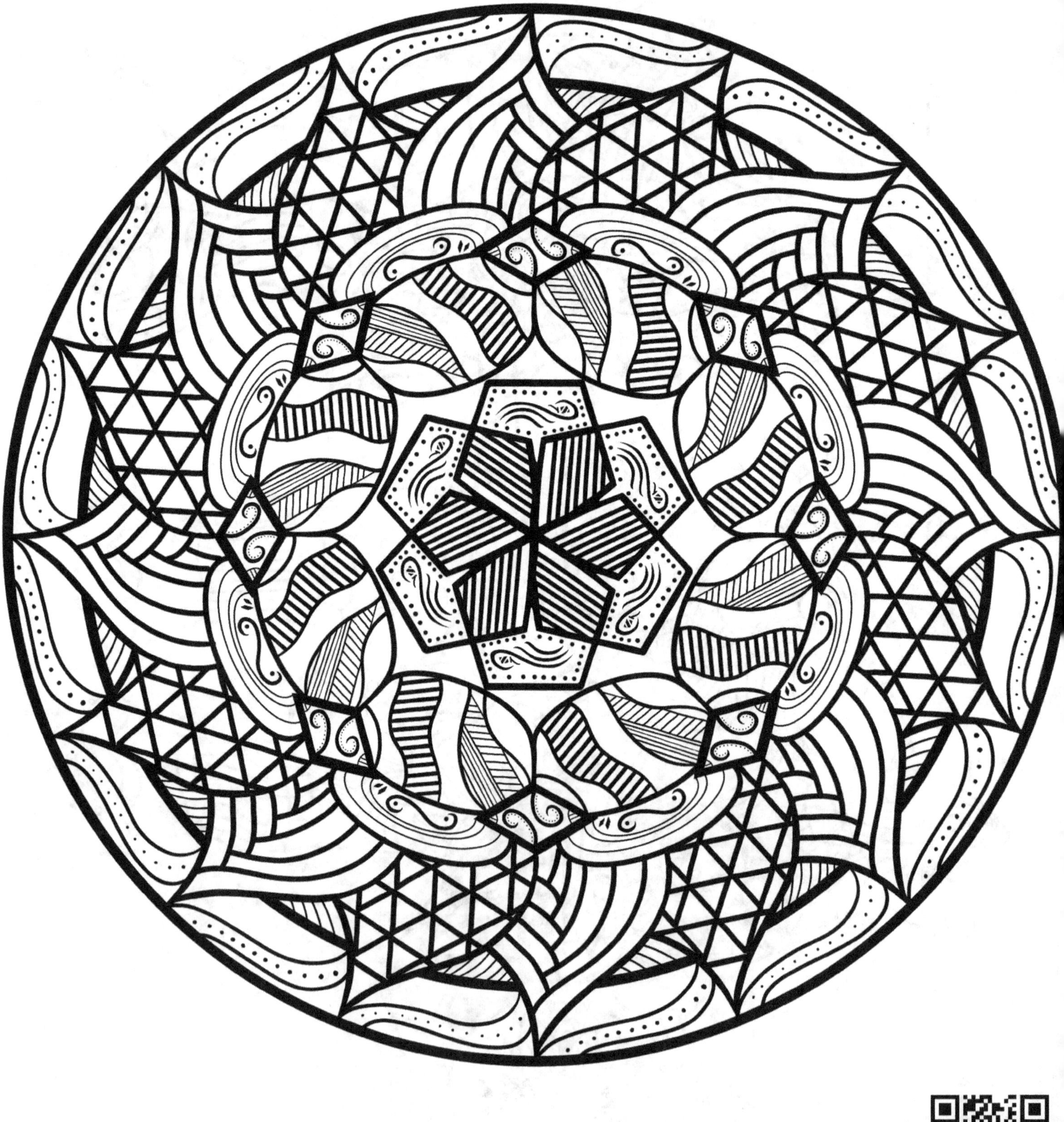

SOLAR STAR

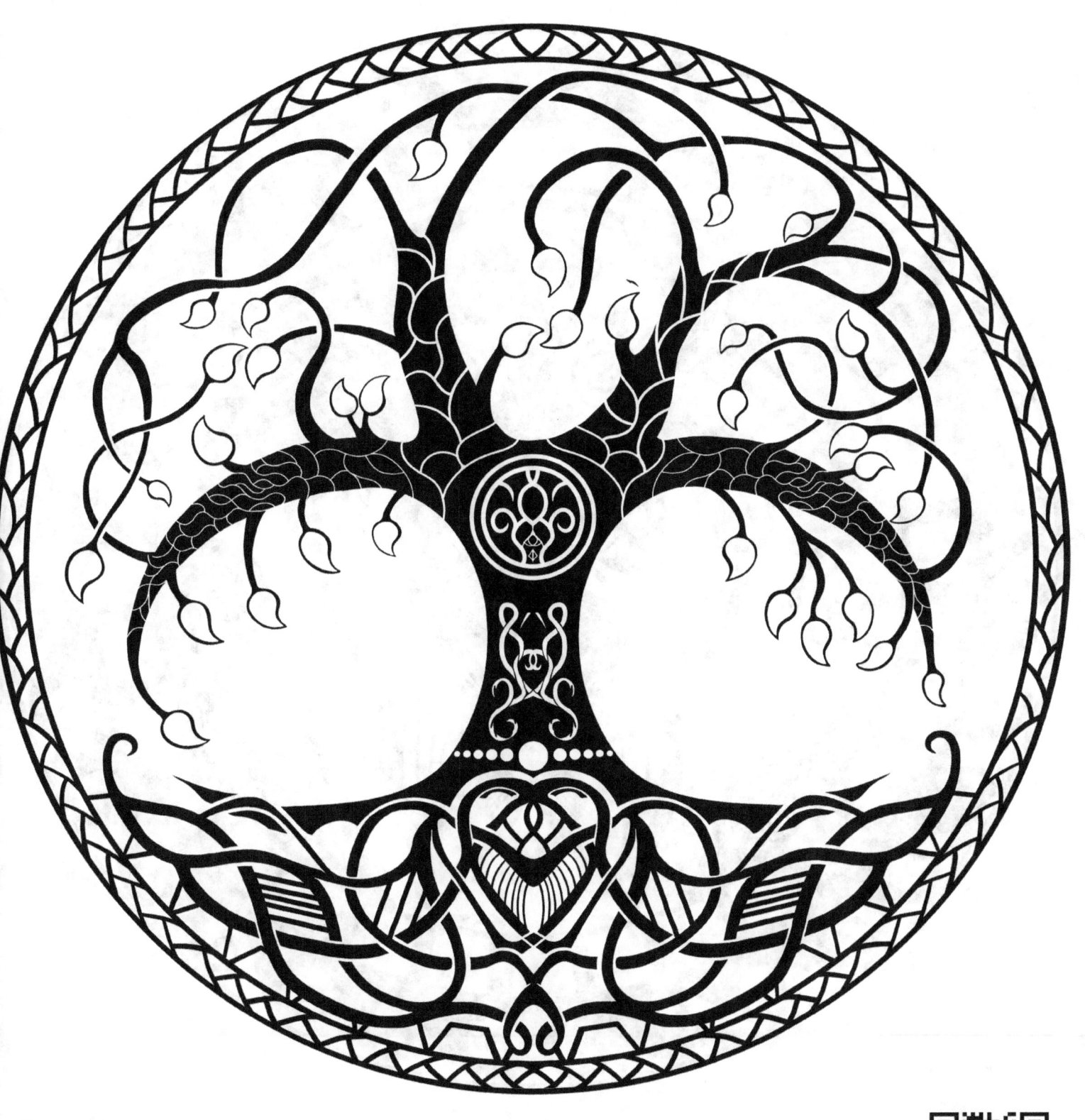

TREE OF LIFE

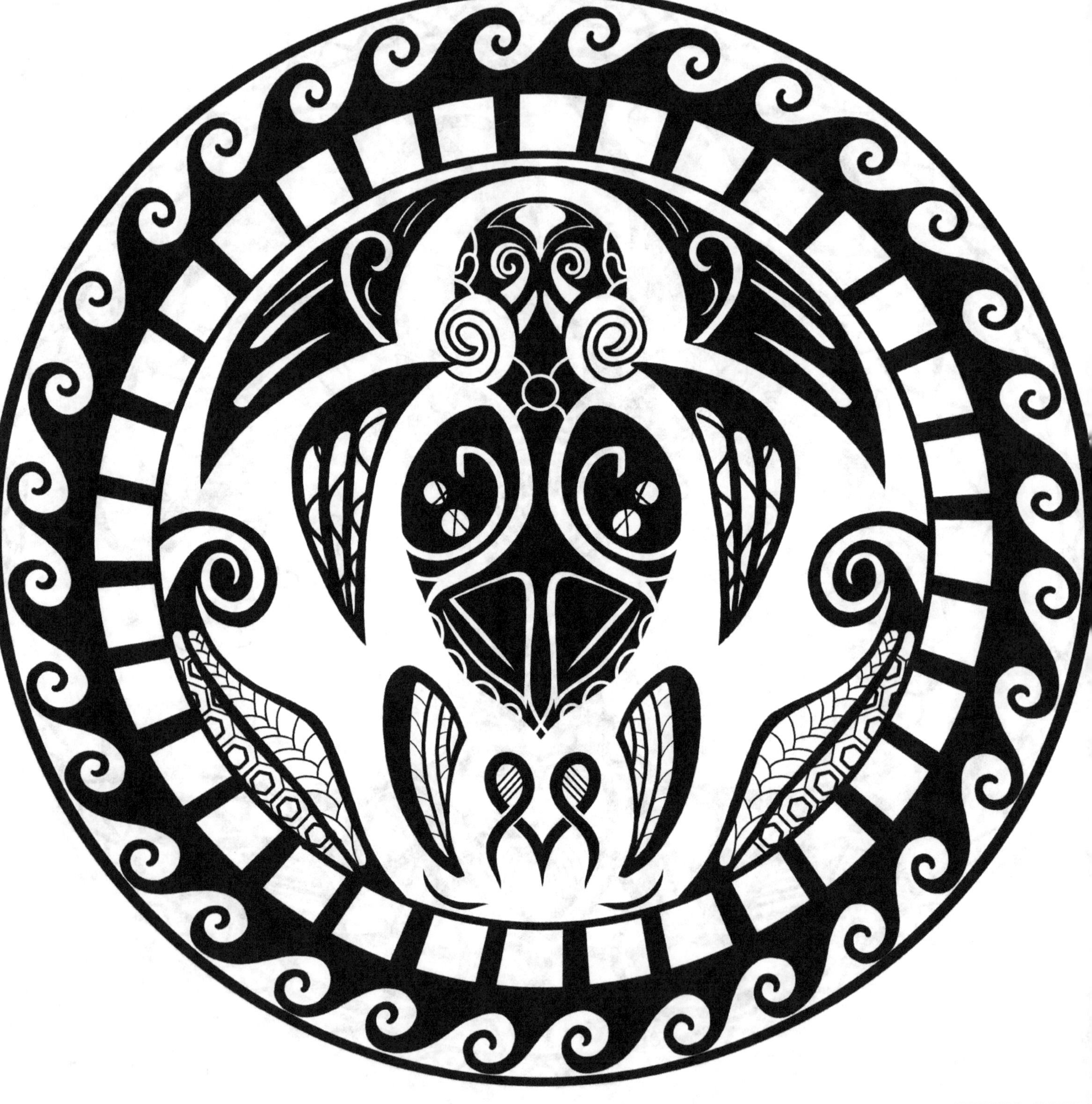

TOPE THE TURTLE

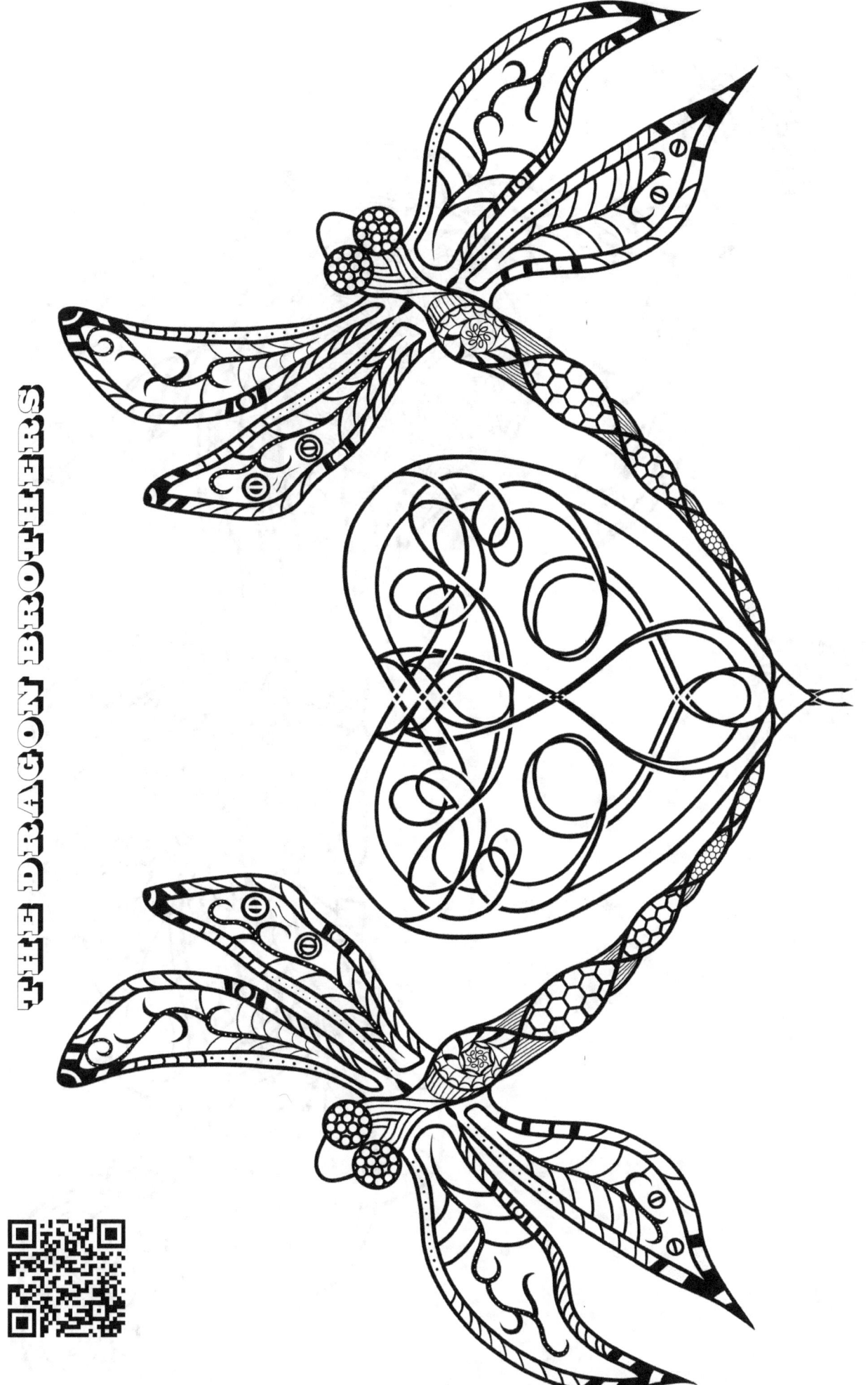

THE DRAGON BROTHERS

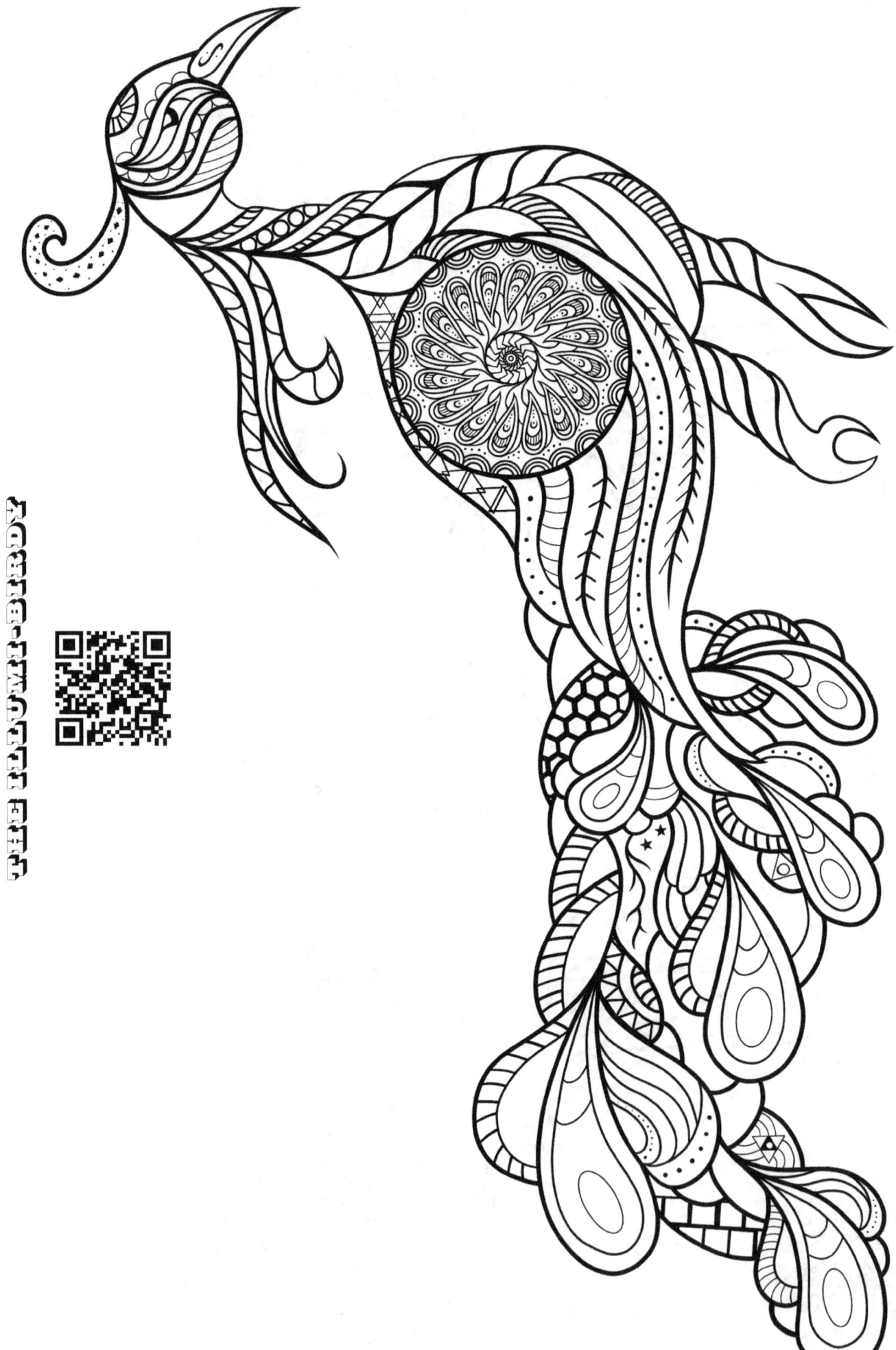

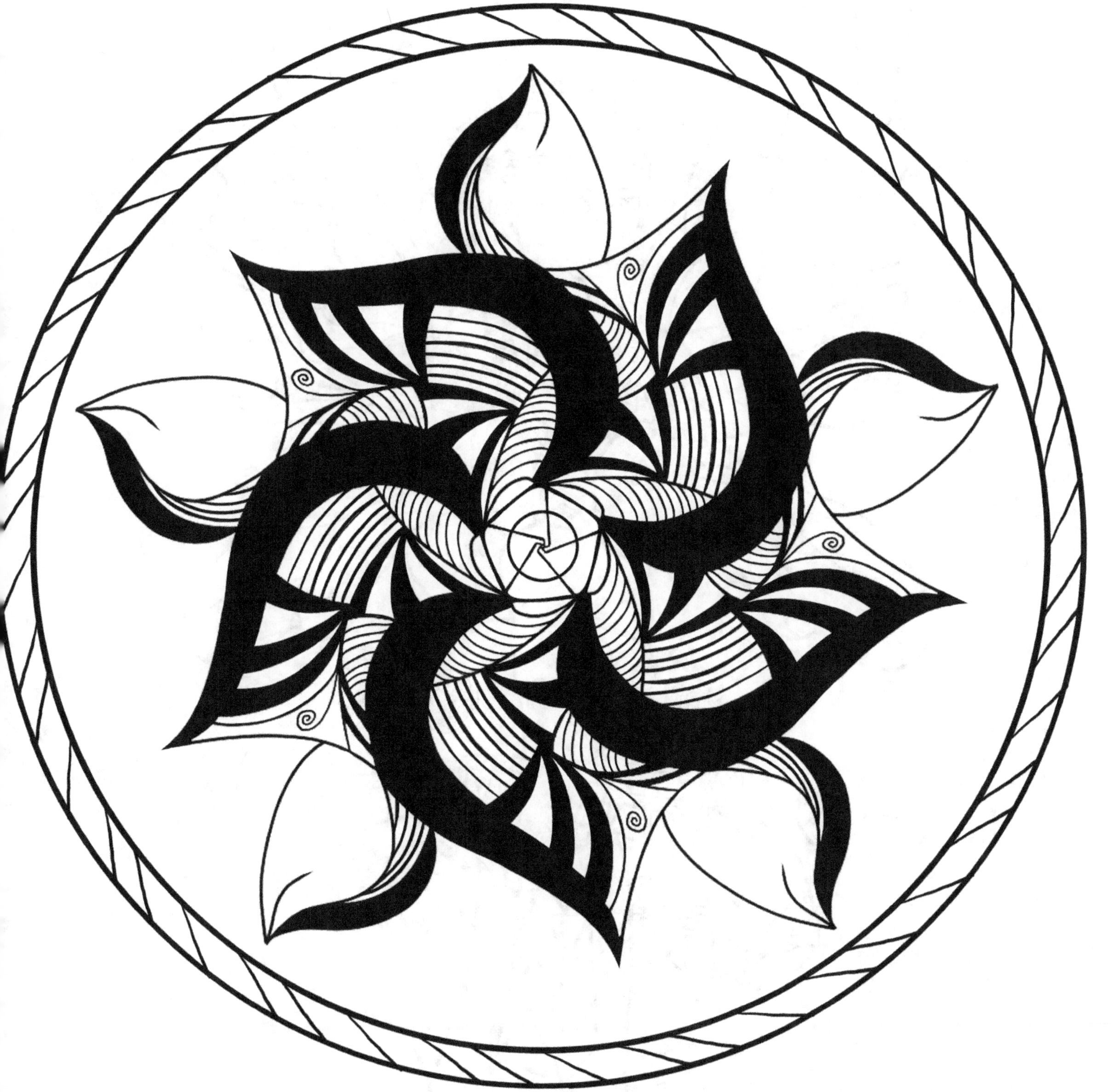

CELTIC ROSE

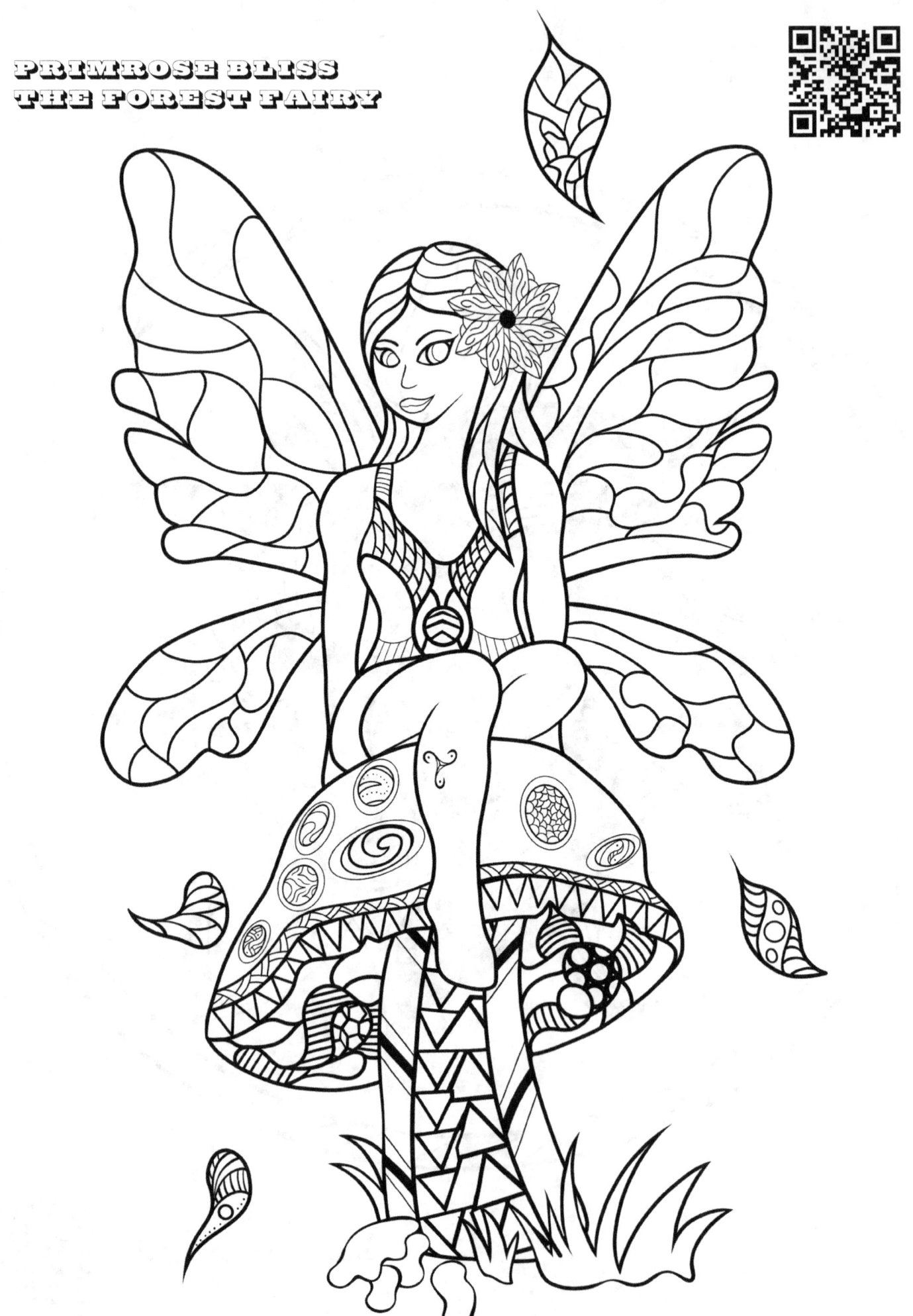

PRIMROSE BLISS
THE FOREST FAIRY

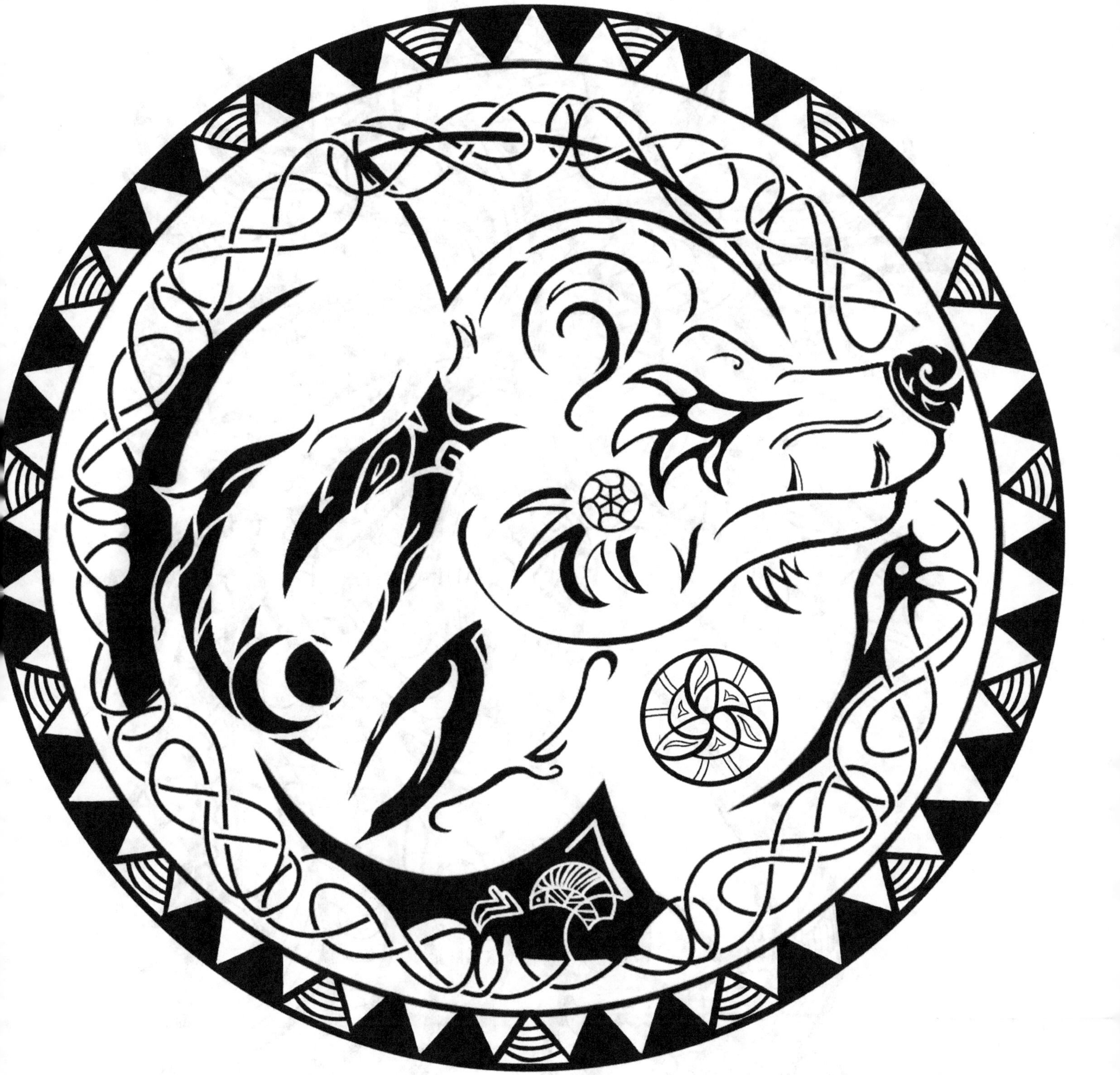

URSANA THE BEAR

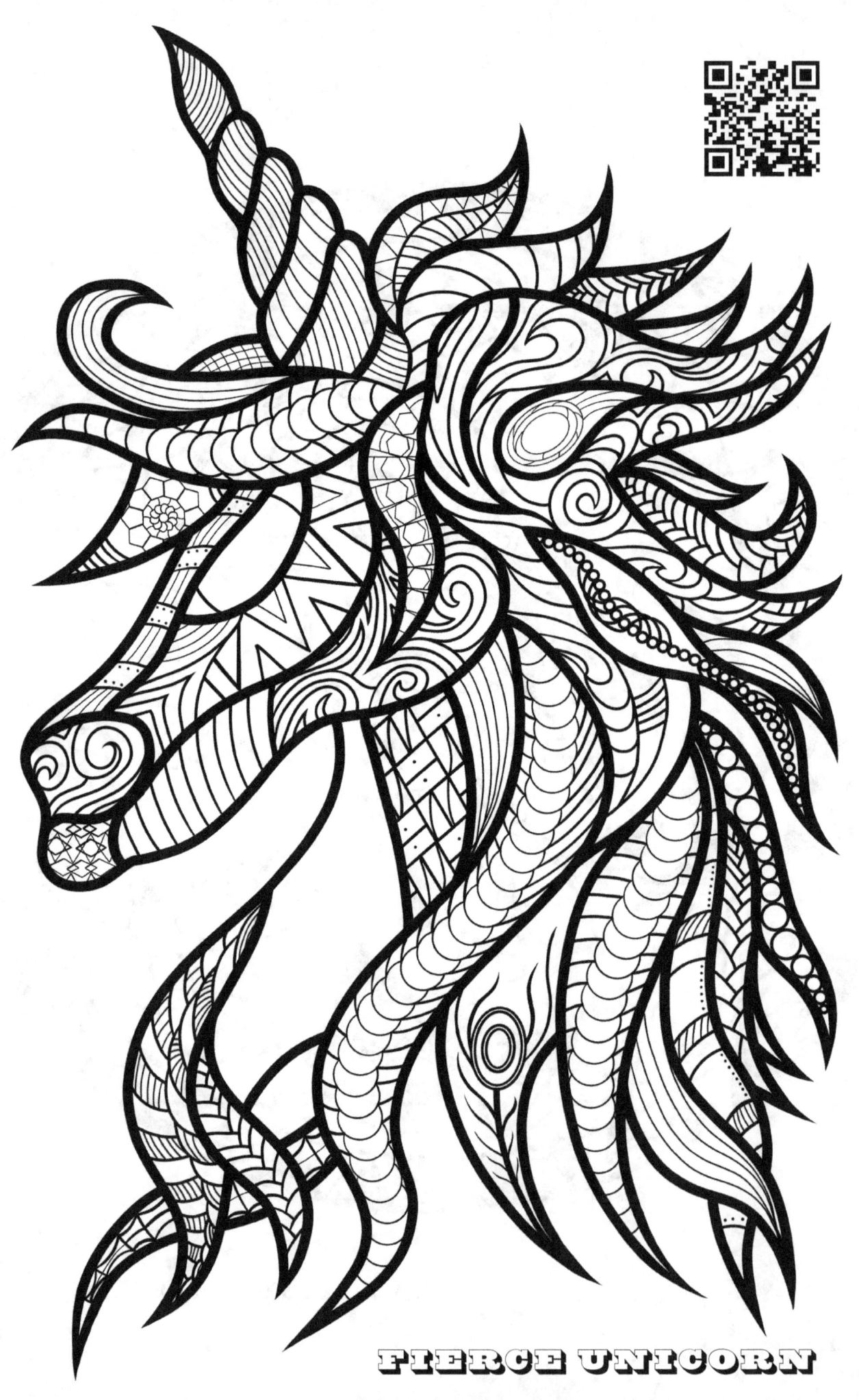

FIERCE UNICORN

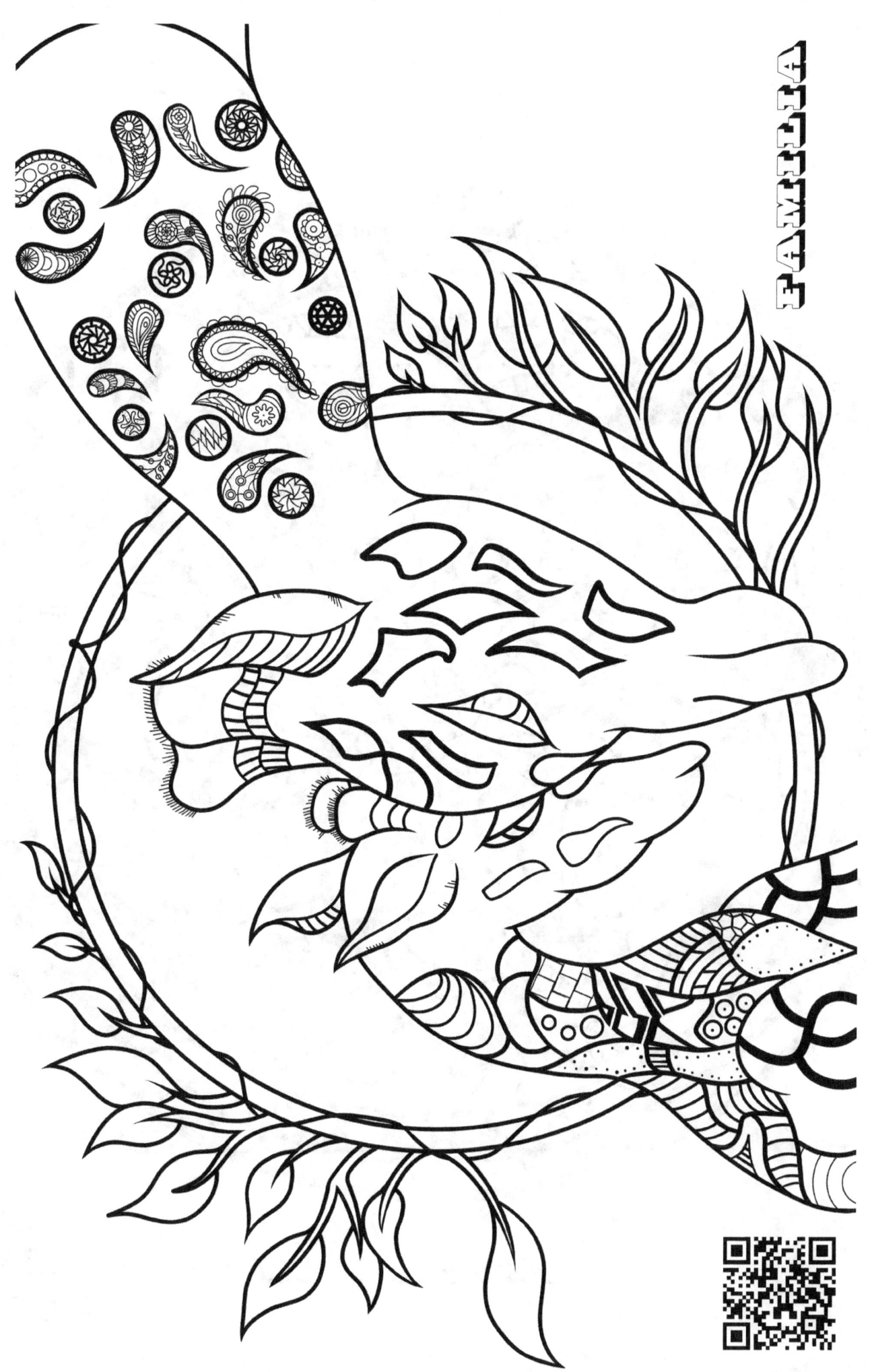

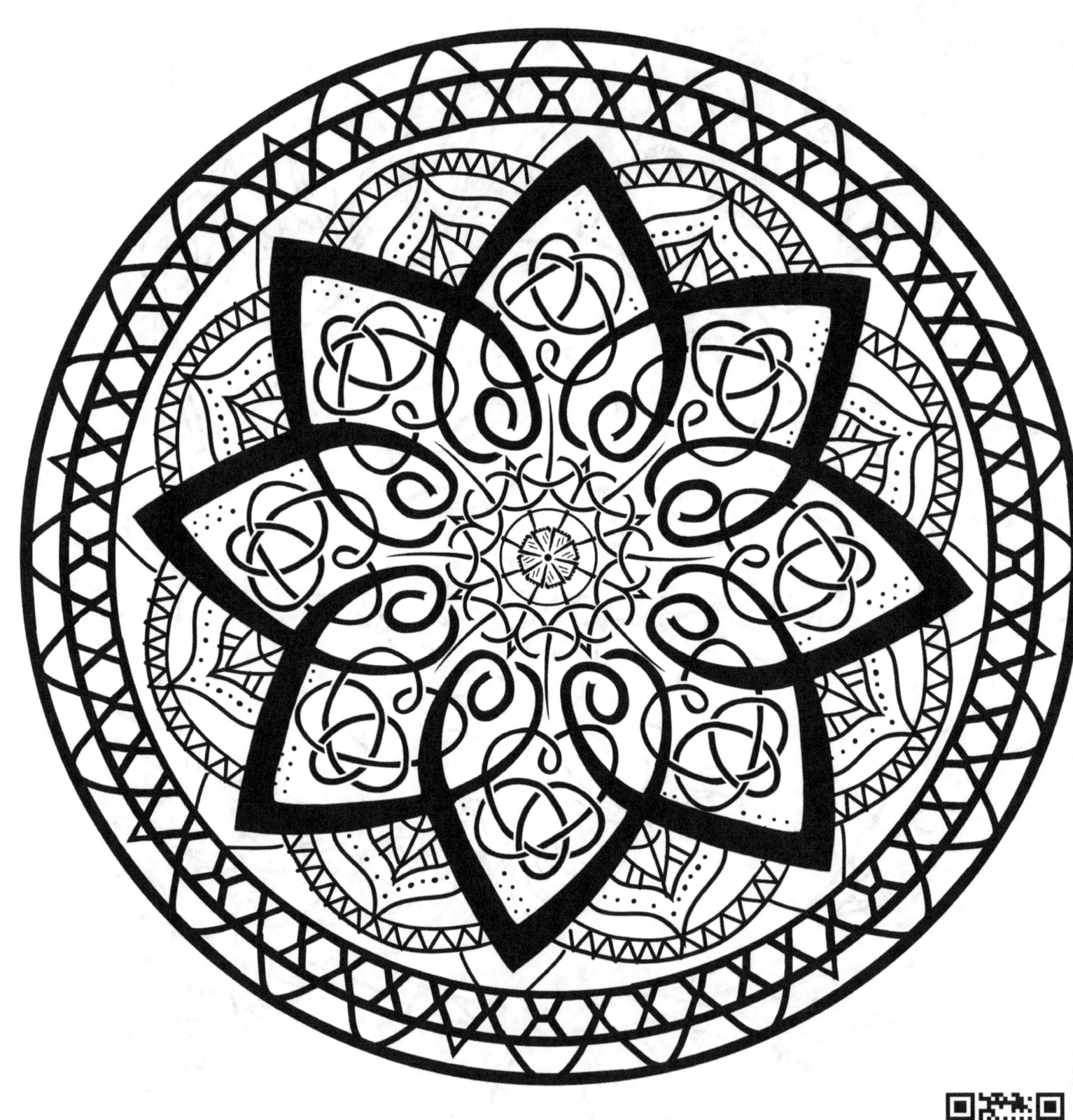

CELTIC MANDALA

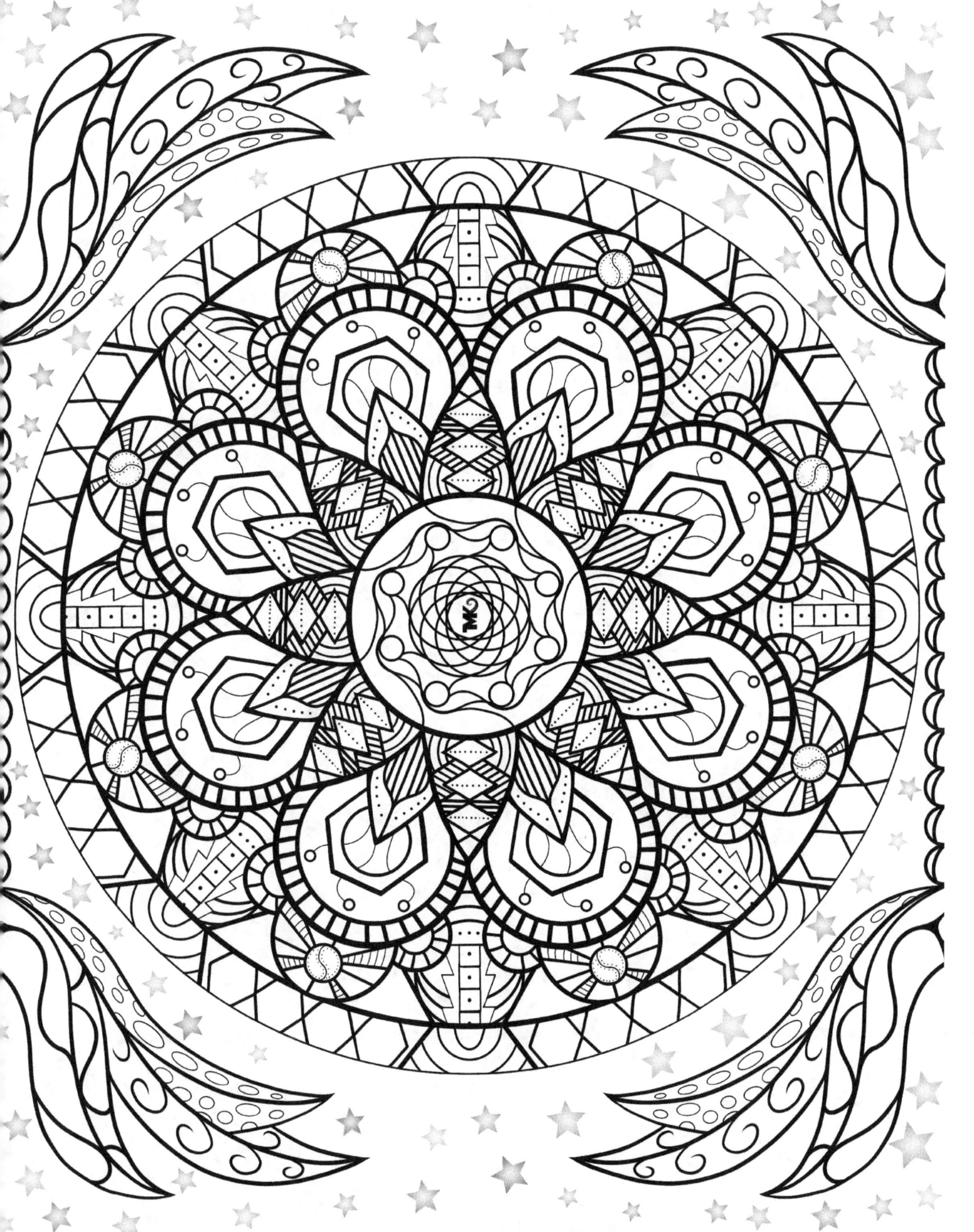